A Trip Thro

Contents

What Time Is It?

You can tell what time it is by
looking at a clock.
But long ago, there were no clocks.
People knew it was day
when the sun was up.
They knew it was night
when it was dark.

But people needed more **accurate** ways to tell the time. They invented different types of **timepieces**.

The Sundial

The **sundial** was one
of the first timepieces.
It was made from a disk
that was divided into sections.
When the sun shone on the piece
in the middle, it made a shadow
on the disk.
The shadow showed what time it was.

This object makes
a shadow.

A section stands
for one hour.

The shadow tells which
hour of the day it is.

People made many different
kinds of sundials.
They all worked the same way.

Time Tidbit

Before sundials, people
poked sticks into the
ground to tell time.

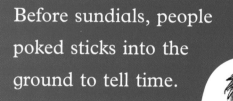

The Water Clock

Some people used **water clocks** to tell time.
Water clocks measured the water that dripped out of a big pot.
A line for each hour was marked inside the smaller pot.
As the water moved up from line to line, people knew how much time had passed.

Greek water clock

Chinese
water clock

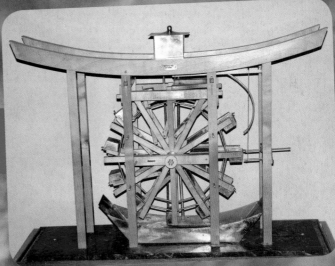

The Hourglass

You may have seen an **hourglass**.
You may even have one
in your home.
But did you know that the hourglass is
thousands of years old?
Instead of using light
to measure time,
this timepiece used sand.

This egg timer works like an hourglass, but it measures minutes instead of an hour.

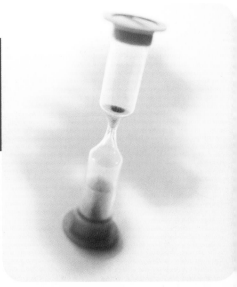

The hourglass was made
of two glass bulbs with
a small space in between.
The top glass bulb
was filled with sand.

When the hourglasss
was turned upside down,
the sand took one hour
to move from the top,
through the middle,
to the bottom.

Mechanical Clocks

A sundial could only be used
on a sunny day.
An hourglass needed someone
to turn it over every hour.
A water clock didn't always
work right.
People needed better ways
to tell time.
They invented **mechanical** clocks,
which worked all the time.
People could depend
on these clocks.

A mechanical clock is one
that uses gears and wheels
to keep more accurate time.
At first, mechanical clocks had
no numbers or hands.

A bell would ring every hour.
Later, hands and numbers were added.

Today, there are many different
kinds of clocks and watches.
All help us answer the question
"What time is it?"

Digital clocks
became popular
after 1975.

Timepiece Timeline

Sundial

3500 BC: first sundial used

Water Clock

270 BC: Ctesibius, an Egyptian barber/inventor, builds a popular water clock

Hourglass

AD 1328: first time an hourglass appears in a painting

Mechanical Clocks

1502: pocket watch invented in Germany

14

 1676: minute hand first appears on clocks

 1680: second hand appears on clocks

 1930s: electric clocks introduced

Digital Clocks

 1975: digital watches introduced

Glossary

accurate: correct

hourglass: a timepiece that uses sand to tell time

mechanical: having to do with machines

sundial: a timepiece that uses the sun to tell time

timepiece: something that shows time

water clock: a timepiece that uses water to tell time